JavaScript

A Detailed Approach to Practical Coding

Nathan Clark

Other Books in this Series

Computer Programming for Beginners

Fundamentals of Programming Terms and Concepts

a FREE Kindle Version with Paperback

JAVASCRIPT

Programming Basics for Absolute Beginners

a FREE Kindle Version with Paperback

JAVASCRIPT

Advanced Features and Programming Techniques

a FREE Kindle Version with Paperback

Table of Contents

Introduction --- 1

1. Loops -- 3

2. Decision Making -- 17

3. Functions --- 29

4. Events in JavaScript ---41

5. Scope in JavaScript --------------------------------------- 45

6. Arrays -- 49

7. Comparisons -- 83

8. Iterators --- 89

9. Maps and Sets -- 93

10. Objects and Properties ------------------------------- 111

11. Methods in JavaScript ------------------------------- 125

12. Form Handling --------------------------------------- 129

13. Multimedia -- 139

Conclusion -- 143

Introduction

This book is the second book in the Step-By-Step JavaScript series. If you are new to JavaScript programming and you haven't read the first book, I highly suggest you do so first. It covers the fundamentals of getting started with JavaScript and takes you step by step through writing your very first program.

JAVASCRIPT

Programming Basics for Absolute Beginners

a. FREE Kindle Version with Paperback

An important aspect of this series, and your learning experience, is **learning by doing**. Practical examples are proven to be the best way to learn a programming language, which is why I have crammed as many examples into this guide as possible. I have tried to keep the core of the examples similar, so the only variable is the topic under discussion. This makes it easier to understand what we are implementing. As you progress through the chapters, remember to follow along with the examples and try them yourself.

1

In this intermediate level guide we will delve more into further concepts of JavaScript. With each topic we will look at a detailed description, proper syntax and numerous examples to make your learning experience as easy as possible. JavaScript is a wonderful programming language and I trust you will enjoy this book as much as I enjoyed writing it.

So without further ado, let's get started!

1. Loops

The usage of loops helps us to iterate through a set of values. Let's say you wanted to to go through a list of students and display their names. Loops can help you to iterate through the list of students easily and can help access each record seperately.

Loops work on a condition and only execute the code based on that condition. A simple view of how this works is shown below.

```
Loop(condition)
{
//Execute code
}
```

So in the above abstract code snippet, we can see that the code will be executed based on the evalaution of the condition in the loop statement. There are different types of loop statements and in this chapter we will go through each of the available loops in more detail.

1.1 While Loops

The general syntax of the while loop is given below.

```
while(condition)
{
//execute code
}
```

While the condition is true in the while loop, the code will continue to execute in the while code block. Let's look at an example of the while statement.

Example 1: The following program is used to showcase how to use the while loop.

```
<!DOCTYPE html>
<html>
<body>
  <h2>JavaScript Program</h2>

  <p id="demo"></p>

  <script>
var text="";
var i=0;
  while (i < 10) {
   text += "The number is " + i + "</br>";
   i++;
}
    document.getElementById("demo").innerHTML = text;

</script>
</body>
</html>
```

Things to note about the above program:

- We are defining an integer 'i' which has an initial value of 0.

4

- In the while loop we state the condition that while the value of 'i' is less than 10, keep on executing the code in the while code block.

- In the while code block, we are appending the value of i to the text of "The number is".

- Finally we set the value of the paragraph block innerHTML to the text value.

With this program, the output is as follows:

JavaScript Program

The number is 0

The number is 1

The number is 2

The number is 3

The number is 4

The number is 5

The number is 6

The number is 7

The number is 8

The number is 9

1.2 do-while Loops

The general syntax of the do-while loop is given below.

```
do
{
//execute code
}
while(condition);
```

The difference between the 'do-while' loop and the normal 'while' loop, is that the condition is tested at the end of the block of code. This means that you will always be guaranteed that the block of code will be executed at least once.

Let's look at an example of the do-while statement.

Example 2: The following program is used to showcase how to use the do-while loop.

```
<!DOCTYPE html>
<html>
<body>
  <h2>JavaScript Program</h2>

  <p id="demo"></p>

  <script>
var text = "";
var i = 0;

do {
  text += "<br>The number is " + i;
  i++;
}
while (i < 10);
document.getElementById("demo").innerHTML = text;

</script>
</body>
</html>
```

Things to note about the above program:

- We are first initializing the value of i to 0.

- In the 'do-while' loop we then set the text variable value. We also then increment the value of 'i'.

- The difference between the 'while' and 'do-while' loop is that the 'do-while' loop will always execute the loop at least once.

- We then execute the statements in the 'do-while' loop until the value of i is less than 10.

With this program, the output is as follows:

JavaScript Program

The number is 0

The number is 1

The number is 2

The number is 3

The number is 4

The number is 5

The number is 6

The number is 7

The number is 8

The number is 9

1.3 for Loops

The general syntax of the for loop is given below.

```
for(initialization;condition;incrementer)
{
//execute code
}
```

In the for clause, you can specify the initialization, condition and incrementer in one statement. Let's look at an example of the for loop statement.

Example 3: The following program is used to showcase how to use the for loop.

```
<!DOCTYPE html>
<html>
<body>
 <h2>JavaScript Program</h2>

  <p id="demo"></p>

  <script>

 for (i = 0; i < 10; i++) {

  text += "The number is " + i +"</br>";
  }

document.getElementById("demo").innerHTML = text;

</script>
</body>
</html>
```

Things to note about the above program:

- We are now initializing the value of 'i' in the for loop itself.

- We are also testing the condition for the value of 'i' in the for loop.

- Next we are incrementing the value of 'i' in the for loop.

8

With this program, the output is as follows:

JavaScript Program

The number is 0

The number is 1

The number is 2

The number is 3

The number is 4

The number is 5

The number is 6

The number is 7

The number is 8

The number is 9

1.4 Nested Loops

We can also nest loops one inside of another. Let's look at some examples of nested loops.

Example 4: The following program is used to showcase how to use nested loops.

```
<!DOCTYPE html>
<html>
<body>
  <h2>JavaScript Program</h2>

  <p id="demo"></p>

  <script>
```

```
var text="";

for(i=0;i<3;i++)
{
for (j = 0; j < 2; j++)
{
  text += "The number is " + j +"</br>";

text += "The number is " + i +"</br>";
}
}
document.getElementById("demo").innerHTML = text;

</script>
</body>
</html>
```

Things to note about the above program:

- We now have 2 'for' loops, one is an outside 'for' loop and the other is an inner 'for' loop.

- For each outer 'for' loop of the 'i' variable, the inner 'for' loop will execute.

With this program, the output is as follows:

JavaScript Program

The number is 0

The number is 0

The number is 1

The number is 0

The number is 0

The number is 1

10

The number is 1

The number is 1

The number is 0

The number is 2

The number is 1

The number is 2

You can also omit the initialization from the for loop if you have declared the variable earlier. Let's look at an example of this.

Example 5: The following program shows how to use a for loop while omitting the initialization.

```
<!DOCTYPE html>
<html>
<body>
  <h2>JavaScript Program</h2>

   <p id="demo"></p>

  <script>

var text="";
var i=0;
for(;i<5;i++)
{
text += "The number is " + i +"</br>";
}
document.getElementById("demo").innerHTML = text;

</script>
</body>
</html>
```

Things to note about the above program:

- In the 'for' loop, we are not initializing the value of 'i'. Instead we are initializing the value before the loop itself.

With this program, the output is as follows:

JavaScript Program

The number is 0

The number is 1

The number is 2

The number is 3

The number is 4

You can also omit the incrementing part from the for loop and increment the value in the loop itself. Let's look at an example of this.

Example 6: The following program shows how to use a for loop while omitting the incrementing portion.

```
<!DOCTYPE html>
<html>
<body>
 <h2>JavaScript Program</h2>

  <p id="demo"></p>

 <script>

var text="";
var i=0;
for(;i<5;)
```

```
{
text += "The number is " + i +"</br>";
i++;
}
document.getElementById("demo").innerHTML = text;

</script>
</body>
</html>
```

Things to note about the above program:

- We are omitting the increment part of the 'for' loop. But remember to increment the value within the 'for' loop itself, or else the loop will go in an infinite cycle.

With this program, the output is as follows:

JavaScript Program

The number is 0

The number is 1

The number is 2

The number is 3

The number is 4

There is also a variation of the for loop which is the for/in loop, which is used to iterate through the properties of an object. Let's look at an example on this.

Example 7: The following program is used to showcase how to use for/in loop.

```html
<!DOCTYPE html>
<html>
<body>
 <h2>JavaScript Program</h2>

  <p id="demo"></p>

 <script>

 var chapters = {1:"Loops", 2:"Decision", 3:"Arrays"};

 var text = "";
 var i;
 for (i in chapters) {
   text += chapters[i];
   text +="</br>";
 }

document.getElementById("demo").innerHTML = text;

</script>
</body>
</html>
```

Things to note about the above program:

- We are defining an object which has 3 elements. Each element has a key and value.

- Next for each element in the 'chapters' object, we use the 'for.in' loop.

- Each index of the element in the 'for.in' loop will be assigned to the variable 'i'.

14

- We can then access each element by means of accessing the chapters object via the index assigned to the variable 'i'.

With this program, the output is as follows:

JavaScript Program

Loops

Decision

Arrays

We can also mix loops by having a while loop inside a for loop. An example is shown below.

Example 8: The following program is used to showcase how to use nested loops.

```html
<!DOCTYPE html>
<html>
<body>
 <h2>JavaScript Program</h2>

  <p id="demo"></p>

 <script>

 var text = "";

 for(i=0;i<3;i++)
  {
  text=text+"The value is "+i;
   text=text+"</br>";
 var j=0;
        while(j<2)
        {
     text=text+"The value is "+j;
```

```
        text=text+"</br>";
            j++;
          }
        }


document.getElementById("demo").innerHTML = text;

</script>
</body>
</html>
```

Things to note about the above program:

- There are 2 loops, one is the outer 'for' loop and the other is the inner 'while' loop.

- For each value in the outer 'for' loop, the inner loop will execute.

With this program, the output is as follows:

JavaScript Program

The value is 0

The value is 0

The value is 1

The value is 1

The value is 0

The value is 1

The value is 2

The value is 0

The value is 1

2. Decision Making

The usage of decision making loops helps us to execute code only if a particular condiion holds true. Let says we wanted to seach for records in a student database and only award scholarships to those students whose aggregate marks were above 90%, then we can use decision loops for this purpose.

A sample decision loop structure is shown below.

```
if(condition)
{
//Execute code
}
```

In the above abstract code snippet, we can see that the code will be executed based on the evalaution of the condition in the 'if' statement. Only if the condition is true then the code block statements will be executed.

There are different types of decision making statements and in this chapter we will go through each of the available statements in more detail.

2.1 if Statement

In the if statement we get the chance to perform an action only if a certain condition evaluates to true. The general syntax of the if statement is given below.

```
if(condition)
{
//Execute code
}
```

Example 9: The following program is used to showcase how to use the if statement.

```
<!DOCTYPE html>
<html>
<body>
 <h2>JavaScript Program</h2>

  <p id="demo"></p>

 <script>

 var text = "";
 var i=5;

 if(i>4)
 {
   text="The value is less than 4";
 }

document.getElementById("demo").innerHTML = text;

</script>
</body>
</html>
```

18

Things to note about the above program:

- • We are defining a condition in the 'if' statement, which says that only if the value of 'i' is greater than 4 will we display the message accordingly.

With this program, the output is as follows:

JavaScript Program

The value is less than 4

2.2 if-else Statement

In the if-else statement we have the option of executing an optional statement if the 'if condition' does not evaluate to true. The general syntax of the if-else statement is given below.

```
if(condition)
{
//Execute code
}
else
{
//Execute code
}
```

Example 10: The following program is used to showcase how to use the if-else statement.

```
<!DOCTYPE html>
<html>
<body>
  <h2>JavaScript Program</h2>
```

```
<p id="demo"></p>

<script>

var text = "";
var i=4;

if(i>5)
{
  text="The value is greater than 5";
}
else {
  text="The value is less than 5";
}

document.getElementById("demo").innerHTML = text;

</script>
</body>
</html>
```

Things to note about the above program:

- We declare a variable of 'i' with a value of 4.

- We then use the 'if' loop. We check the value of 'i' and whether it is less than 5.

- If the value is greater than 5, the code block will be executed in the 'else' block.

With this program, the output is as follows:

JavaScript Program

The value is less than 5

2.3 else if Statement

The else if statement is used to specify a new condition if the first condition is false.

```
if (condition1)
{
   //Execute code
}
else if (condition2)
{
   //Execute code
}
else
{
   //Execute code
}
```

Example 11: The following program is used to showcase how to use the else if statement.

```
<!DOCTYPE html>
<html>
<body>
  <h2>JavaScript Program</h2>

   <p id="demo"></p>

  <script>

  var text = "";
  var i=16;

  if (i >20 ) {
    text="The value is greater than 20";
  } else if (i > 10) {
    text="The value is greater than 10";
```

21

```
} else {
   text="The value is greater than 5";
}

document.getElementById("demo").innerHTML = text;

</script>
</body>
</html>
```

Things to note about the above program:

- This time around, we have an inner 'if' statement. So if the value of the variable 'i' is less than 20, then the 'else if' loop will execute.

- And if the value of 'i' is less than 10, then the final else statement will execute.

With this program, the output is as follows:

JavaScript Program

The value is greater than 10

2.4 switch Statement

The switch statement helps us to evaluate multiple options at once and then execute code based on those various options. The general syntax of the switch statement is given below.

```
switch(expression) {
  case constant-expression :
    statement(s);
    break;
```

```
    case constant-expression :
      statement(s);
      break;

    default :
    statement(s);
}
```

In the switch statement, you can evaluate the condition against multiple expressions. For each matching expression you can have the corresponding statements to execute. Once the statement is found, the break statement helps to exit from the switch statement.

You can also have a default statement which gets executed if neither of the expressions matches the condition in the switch statement.

Example 12: The following program is used to showcase how to use the switch statement.

```
<!DOCTYPE html>
<html>
<body>
 <h2>JavaScript Program</h2>

  <p id="demo"></p>

 <script>

var input=3;
var number="";
 switch (input) {
   case 1:
     number = "One";
     break;
```

```
    case 2:
      number = "Two";
      break;

    case 3:
      number = "Three";
      break;

    }
document.getElementById("demo").innerHTML = number;

</script>
</body>
</html>
```

Things to note about the above program:

- We are defining the switch statement to evaluate the input value.

- We are defining the different possible values of input using the case statements.

With this program, the output is as follows:

JavaScript Program

Three

Example 13: The following program shows how to use the switch statement with the default statement.

```
<!DOCTYPE html>
<html>
<body>
  <h2>JavaScript Program</h2>
```

```
<p id="demo"></p>

<script>

var input=4;
var number="";
 switch (input) {
   case 1:
      number = "One";
      break;

   case 2:
      number = "Two";
      break;

   case 3:
      number = "Three";
      break;

default:
      number="Invalid number";
    }
document.getElementById("demo").innerHTML = number;

</script>
</body>
</html>
```

Things to note about the above program:

- The 'input' variable value will become an input to the switch statement.

- Each case statement will be checked for the value of the variable 'input'.

- If any value does not match, then the code in the default block will execute.

With this program, the output is as follows:

JavaScript Program

Invalid number

2.5 Nested Statements

We can also make use of nested statements. Let's look at some examples of nested statements.

Example 14: The following program shows how to use the nested decision making statements.

```
<!DOCTYPE html>
<html>
<body>
  <h2>JavaScript Program</h2>

   <p id="demo"></p>

  <script>

var i=4;
var text="";
if (i > 0)
{
 if (i == 4)
 {
    text=text+"The value is 4";
 }
}
```

```
document.getElementById("demo").innerHTML = text;

</script>
</body>
</html>
```

In the above program we are making use of multiple if statements in the program.

With this program, the output is as follows:

JavaScript Program

The value is 4

Let's look at another example of using nested decision making statements.

Example 15: The following program also shows how to use the nested decision making statements.

```
<!DOCTYPE html>
<html>
<body>
  <h2>JavaScript Program</h2>

   <p id="demo"></p>

   <script>

var input=3;
var number="";
if (input>0)
{
  switch (input) {
    case 1:
```

```
      number = "One";
      break;

   case 2:
      number = "Two";
      break;

   case 3:
      number = "Three";
      break;

default:
      number="Invalid number";
     }
   }
document.getElementById("demo").innerHTML = number;

</script>
</body>
</html>
```

With this program, the output is as follows:

JavaScript Program

Three

3. Functions

Functions are used to define a set of logical statements together. This set of statements are used for a definitive purpose. For example if you wanted to add a set of numbers together, you can define a method for that and call the method whenever you wanted to add numbers.

The general syntax of a method is shown below.

```
function functionName(parameters)
{
// Code to be executed
}
```

Where:

- The function is defined by the function keyword.

- The function has a name attached to it.

- The function can be passed parameters for processing.

Let's now look at a simple example of how to define a function and call the function accordingly.

Example 16: The following program is used to showcase how to use functions.

```
<!DOCTYPE html>
<html>
<body>
  <h2>JavaScript Program</h2>

   <p id="demo"></p>

  <script>
var i;
  function demofunction(a, b) {
    i=a*b;
  }

  demofunction(2, 5);
document.getElementById("demo").innerHTML = i;

</script>
</body>
</html>
```

With this program, the output is as follows:

JavaScript Program

10

3.1 Storing Functions in Expressions

Functions can also be stored in expressions as shown below.

```
function functionName(parameters)
{
// Code to be executed
}
Var varname=functionName
```

30

Let's look at an example of this.

Example 17: The following program is used to showcase how to use functions with expressions.

```
<!DOCTYPE html>
<html>
<body>
  <h2>JavaScript Program</h2>

  <p id="demo"></p>

  <script>
var i;
var x;
  x=function demofunction(a, b) {
    i=a*b;
  }

  x(2, 5);
document.getElementById("demo").innerHTML = i;

</script>
</body>
</html>
```

Things to note about the above program:

- We are declaring a function which takes in 2 parameters.

- We then multiply the values provided in the function.

- Then we call the function by passing in the value of 2 and 5.

31

With this program, the output is as follows:

JavaScript Program

10

3.2 Declaring Functions with Constructors

A function in JavaScript can also be declared using the built-in JavaScript functions. Let's look at an example of this.

The syntax for this is shown below.

```
var varname = new Function(//Code to be executed);
```

Where:

- The 'varname' is the name of the variable.

- The 'new' keyword is used to define a new function.

- In the function, we define the code that needs to be executed.

Example 18: The following program is used to showcase how to use functions with constructors.

```
<!DOCTYPE html>
<html>
<body>
  <h2>JavaScript Program</h2>

  <p id="demo"></p>
```

```
  <script>
var i;
var x;

var x = new Function("a", "b", "i=a*b");
var y = x(4, 3);


document.getElementById("demo").innerHTML = i;

</script>
</body>
</html>
```

Things to note about the above program:

- We use the 'function' keyword to create a new function. The first 2 parameters of 'a' and 'b' are used to specify the parameters for the function.

- The next parameter is the code that becomes the block of code for the function.

With this program, the output is as follows:

JavaScript Program

12

3.3 Functions Returning Values

Functions can also be used to return values to the main program. The format of this function is given below.

```
function functionName(parameters)
{
// Code to be executed
return value;
}
```

The return value will be returned to the calling program. Let's look at an example of this.

Example 19: The following program is used to showcase how to use functions with return values.

```
<!DOCTYPE html>
<html>
<body>
  <h2>JavaScript Program</h2>

    <p id="demo"></p>

  <script>


function demofunction(a, b) {
    return a*b;
 }


document.getElementById("demo").innerHTML =
demofunction(5,2);

</script>
</body>
</html>
```

Things to note about the above program:

- We are returning the result of multiplying the values of 'a' and 'b' to the main calling program.

With this program, the output is as follows:

JavaScript Program

10

The output of JavaScript functions can also be used in expressions. Let's look at an example below.

Example 20: The following program is used to showcase how to use functions with expressions.

```
<!DOCTYPE html>
<html>
<body>
 <h2>JavaScript Program</h2>

  <p id="demo"></p>

 <script>


function demofunction(a, b) {
    return a*b;
 }

 var x=demofunction(5,2)+2;
document.getElementById("demo").innerHTML = x;

</script>
</body>
</html>
```

With this program, the output is as follows:

JavaScript Program

12

You can also get the number of arguments defined in the function. An example is shown below.

Example 21: The following program shows how to utilize the number of arguments.

```
<!DOCTYPE html>
<html>
<body>
 <h2>JavaScript Program</h2>
   <p id="demo"></p>
  <script>
function demofunction(a, b) {
    return arguments.length;
 }

document.getElementById("demo").innerHTML =
demofunction(5,2);

</script>
</body>
</html>
```

Things to note about the above program:

- In the function 'demofunction' which accepts 2 parameters 'a' and 'b', the arguments.length will return the value of 2.

With this program, the output is as follows:

JavaScript Program

2

If the number of arguments passed to a function is less than the number of arguments defined, then the parameter is given the value of 'undefined'. An example is shown below.

Example 22: The following program is used to showcase how to use functions with undefined arguments.

```
<!DOCTYPE html>
<html>
<body>
  <h2>JavaScript Program</h2>

   <p id="demo"></p>

  <script>


function demofunction(a, b) {
 if (b === undefined) {
    b = 0;
}
return b;
 }


document.getElementById("demo").innerHTML =
demofunction(5);

</script>
</body>
</html>
```

With this program, the output is as follows:

JavaScript Program

0

One can also iterate through the values passed as parameters, just like with an object. Hence you can have a function that accepts no parameters and still be able to pass values, and then access those values via the argument object. Let's look at an example shown below.

Example 23: The following program is used to showcase how to use functions with argument objects.

```
<!DOCTYPE html>
<html>
<body>
 <h2>JavaScript Program</h2>

  <p id="demo"></p>

  <script>

var text="";
function demofunction() {
 for (i = 0; i < arguments.length; i++) {
    text+="The value is "+arguments[i]+"</br>";
 }
}
 demofunction(5,6,7,8);
document.getElementById("demo").innerHTML = text;

</script>
</body>
</html>
```

Things to note about the above program:

- The 'demofunction' takes in 4 parameters of 5, 6, 7 and 8.

- We can then iterate through the argument collection to get the values of the parameters passed to the 'demofunction' function.

With this program, the output is as follows:

JavaScript Program

The value is 5

The value is 6

The value is 7

The value is 8

3.4 Functions as Object Methods

Functions can also be used as object methods. Let's look at example of this to understand this in further detail.

Example 24: The following program is used to showcase how to use functions as object methods.

```
<!DOCTYPE html>
<html>
<body>
  <h2>JavaScript Program</h2>

    <p id="demo"></p>

  <script>

var numbers = {
    first:1,
    second: 2,
```

```
    add: function () {
        return this.first*this.second;
    }
}

document.getElementById("demo").innerHTML = numbers.add();

</script>
</body>
</html>
```

Things to note about the above program:

- The 'numbers' object has an extra key of 'add'. The value is an entire definition of a function that is used to multiply the values of the keys 'first' and 'second'.

- The value of the keys 'first' and 'second' can be acquired from the 'this' keyword.

- We then call the function via the object 'number'.

With this program, the output is as follows:

JavaScript Program

2

4. Events in JavaScript

Events are aspects which occur in a program. Code can be executed whenever an event is triggered in the HTML program. For example, if a button is clicked on an HTML page, an event is triggered and a function can be executed based on this trigger. Let's look at a simple example of this.

Some of the HTML events are shown below.

Event	Description
Onchange	An HTML element has been changed
Onclick	The user clicks an HTML element
Onmouseover	The user moves the mouse over an HTML element
Onmouseout	The user moves the mouse away from an HTML element
Onkeydown	The user pushes a keyboard key
Onload	The browser has finished loading the page

Example 25: The following program is used to showcase how to use triggers.

```
<!DOCTYPE html>
<html>
<body>
 <h2>JavaScript Program</h2>
    <p id="demo"></p>
<button onclick="document.getElementById('demo').innerHTML =
1">Hello</button>
 <script>
 </script>
</body>
</html>
```

Things to note about the above program:

- The button HTML tag has an event called 'onclick' which is called whenever the button is clicked.

- When the button is clicked, we then change the value of the innerHTML property of the 'demo' element.

With this program, the output is as follows:

When you click on the Hello button you will get the following output.

JavaScript Program

1

Let's look at an example of how we can use triggers with functions.

Example 26: The following program is used to showcase how to use triggers with functions.

```
<!DOCTYPE html>
<html>
<body>
  <h2>JavaScript Program</h2>

  <p id="demo"></p>

<button onclick="demofunction()">Hello</button>

  <script>

function demofunction()
{
document.getElementById("demo").innerHTML = 1;
}
</script>
</body>
</html>
```

Things to note about the above program:

- This time around we are defining a function called 'demofunction'. This function gets called whenever the button gets clicked.

With this program, the output is as follows:

When you click on the Hello button you will get the following output.

JavaScript Program

1

Hello

5. Scope in JavaScript

J ust like with any programming language, the variables in JavaScript also have a scope defined for them. This scope details where the variables can be accessed from.

For example, in the sample code below, the x and y variables both have different scopes. The variable 'y' has the scope only defined to the function, because it is defined in this scope. Hence the scope of the variable 'y' is local to that block of code. Alternatively the variable 'x' has a global scope and can be used anywhere in the scope of the entire JavaScript program.

```
var x;
Function demo() {
var y;
```

Let's look at an example of how the scope works.

Example 27: The following program shows how the scope in JavaScript works without functions.

```
<!DOCTYPE html>
<html>
<body>
  <h2>JavaScript Program</h2>
```

```
    <p id="inner"></p>
    <p id="outer"></p>
<script>
var x=5;
{
  var y=6;
}
document.getElementById("inner").innerHTML = y;
document.getElementById("outer").innerHTML = x;
</script>
</body>
</html>
```

The following needs to be noted about the above program:

- Both variables are defined at different points in the program, but they can be accessed anywhere.

With this program, the output is as follows:

JavaScript Program

6

5

Now let's look at an example where scope is seperated via functions.

Example 28: The following program shows how the scope in JavaScript works with functions.

```
<!DOCTYPE html>
<html>
<body>
  <h2>JavaScript Program</h2>
```

46

```
  <p id="inner"></p>
  <p id="outer"></p>
<script>
var x=5;
function demo()
{
 var y=6;
 document.getElementById("inner").innerHTML = y;
}
demo();
document.getElementById("outer").innerHTML = x;
</script>
</body>
</html>
```

The following needs to be noted about the above program:

- Since the variable 'y' is declared in the function demo(), the document.getElementById("inner").innerHTML statement using the value of 'y' needs to be in the function, in order for it to work. Since the scope of the variable 'y' is local to the function, the value is only valid in the function itself.

With this program, the output is as follows:

JavaScript Program

6

5

6. Arrays

Arrays are used to define a collection of values of a similar datatype. The definition of a data type is shown below. As an example, let's say we wanted to define 3 numbers that serve the same purpose as shown below.

```
var x=1;
var y=2;
var z=3;
```

Instead of defining 3 variables, we can just define an array.

```
var x=[1,2,3]
```

Here we are defining just one variable with 3 values. The values of the array can be accessed via the index numbers as shown below.

- x[0] – This will access the first element of the array.

- x[1] – This will access the second element of the array.

- x[2] – This will access the third element of the array.

Let's now look at an example of how we can define an array in JavaScript.

Example 29: The following program is used to showcase how arrays can be used.

```
<!DOCTYPE html>
<html>
<body>
  <h2>JavaScript Program</h2>

  <p id="x1"></p>
  <p id="x2"></p>
  <p id="x3"></p>
<script>
var x=[1,2,3];
document.getElementById("x1").innerHTML = x[0];
document.getElementById("x2").innerHTML = x[1];
document.getElementById("x3").innerHTML = x[2];
</script>
</body>
</html>
```

Things to note about the above program:

- We are defining an array called 'x' with 3 values.

- We then access each value via the array name and the index number.

With this program, the output is as follows:

JavaScript Program

1

2

3

The values of each value in the array can also be changed. Let's look at an example of this.

Example 30: The following program shows how arrays can be used to change values.

```
<!DOCTYPE html>
<html>
<body>
 <h2>JavaScript Program</h2>

  <p id="x1"></p>
  <p id="x2"></p>
  <p id="x3"></p>

  <p id="x11"></p>
  <p id="x22"></p>
  <p id="x33"></p>

<script>
var x=[1,2,3];

document.getElementById("x1").innerHTML = x[0];
document.getElementById("x2").innerHTML = x[1];
document.getElementById("x3").innerHTML = x[2];
x[0]=4;
x[1]=5;
x[2]=6;

document.getElementById("x11").innerHTML = x[0];
document.getElementById("x22").innerHTML = x[1];
document.getElementById("x33").innerHTML = x[2];

</script>
</body>
</html>
```

Things to note about the above program:

- We first define the array with 3 values.

- We then change the values via the index of the array.

With this program, the output is as follows:

JavaScript Program

1

2

3

4

5

6

Arrays can also be used to hold values of different data types. Let's look at an example of this.

Example 31: The following program shows how arrays can be used to hold different values.

```
<!DOCTYPE html>
<html>
<body>
 <h2>JavaScript Program</h2>

  <p id="x1"></p>
  <p id="x2"></p>
  <p id="x3"></p>

  <p id="x11"></p>
  <p id="x22"></p>
  <p id="x33"></p>
```

```
<script>
var x=["demo1","demo2","demo3"];

document.getElementById("x1").innerHTML = x[0];
document.getElementById("x2").innerHTML = x[1];
document.getElementById("x3").innerHTML = x[2];
x[0]="demo4";
x[1]="demo5";
x[2]="demo6";

document.getElementById("x11").innerHTML = x[0];
document.getElementById("x22").innerHTML = x[1];
document.getElementById("x33").innerHTML = x[2];

</script>
</body>
</html>
```

With this program, the output is as follows:

JavaScript Program

demo1

demo2

demo3

demo4

demo5

demo6

The JavaScript loops can also be used to iterate through the values of the array. Let's look at an example on this.

Example 32: The following program shows how loops can be used to iterate through the values of an array.

```
<!DOCTYPE html>
<html>
<body>
  <h2>JavaScript Program</h2>

  <p id="x1"></p>
  <p id="x2"></p>
  <p id="x3"></p>

  <p id="x11"></p>
  <p id="x22"></p>
  <p id="x33"></p>

<script>
var x=["demo1","demo2","demo3"];
var text="";
for(i=0;i<3;i++)
{
 text+=x[i];
 text+="</br>";
}
document.getElementById("x1").innerHTML = x[0];
document.getElementById("x2").innerHTML = x[1];
document.getElementById("x3").innerHTML = x[2];

</script>
</body>
</html>
```

With this program, the output is as follows:

JavaScript Program

demo1

demo2

demo3

You can also display all the elements of an array at one. Let's look at an example of this.

Example 33: The following program shows how to display all the elements of an array at once.

```
<!DOCTYPE html>
<html>
<body>
  <h2>JavaScript Program</h2>

    <p id="demo"></p>

<script>
var x=["demo1","demo2","demo3"];

document.getElementById("demo").innerHTML = x;

</script>
</body>
</html>
```

With this program, the output is as follows:

JavaScript Program

demo1,demo2,demo3

6.1 Length of the Array

The length of the array can be determined with the 'length' property of the array. Let's look at an example of this.

Example 34: The following program is used to showcase how to use the length property.

```
<!DOCTYPE html>
<html>
<body>
  <h2>JavaScript Program</h2>

  <p id="demo"></p>

<script>
var x=["demo1","demo2","demo3"];

document.getElementById("demo").innerHTML = x.length;

</script>
</body>
</html>
```

With this program, the output is as follows:

JavaScript Program

3

6.2 Sorting the Array

The elements of an array can also be sorted. Let's look at an example of this.

56

Example 35: The following program is used to showcase how to use the sort function.

```
<!DOCTYPE html>
<html>
<body>
 <h2>JavaScript Program</h2>

  <p id="x1"></p>
  <p id="x2"></p>
  <p id="x3"></p>

  <p id="x11"></p>
  <p id="x22"></p>
  <p id="x33"></p>

<script>
var x=[3,2,1];

document.getElementById("x1").innerHTML = x[0];
document.getElementById("x2").innerHTML = x[1];
document.getElementById("x3").innerHTML = x[2];

x.sort();
document.getElementById("x11").innerHTML = x[0];
document.getElementById("x22").innerHTML = x[1];
document.getElementById("x33").innerHTML = x[2];

</script>
</body>
</html>
```

With this program, the output is as follows:

JavaScript Program

3
2
1
1
2
3

This feature also works if the elements of an array are of the 'string' data type. Let's look at an example of this.

Example 36: The following program shows how to use the sort function with strings as array elements.

```
<!DOCTYPE html>
<html>
<body>
 <h2>JavaScript Program</h2>

  <p id="x1"></p>
  <p id="x2"></p>
  <p id="x3"></p>

  <p id="x11"></p>
  <p id="x22"></p>
  <p id="x33"></p>

<script>
var x=["C","B","A"];

document.getElementById("x1").innerHTML = x[0];
document.getElementById("x2").innerHTML = x[1];
document.getElementById("x3").innerHTML = x[2];
```

```
x.sort();
document.getElementById("x11").innerHTML = x[0];
document.getElementById("x22").innerHTML = x[1];
document.getElementById("x33").innerHTML = x[2];

</script>
</body>
</html>
```

With this program, the output is as follows:

JavaScript Program

C
B
A
A
B
C

6.3 Adding Elements to the Array

Elements can be added to the array with the 'push' function. Let's look at an example of how this can be accomplished.

Example 37: The following program is used to showcase how to add elements to the array.

```
<!DOCTYPE html>
<html>
<body>
  <h2>JavaScript Program</h2>

  <p id="x1"></p>
```

59

```
   <p id="x2"></p>
   <p id="x3"></p>
   <p id="x4"></p>

<script>
var x=[1,2,3];

document.getElementById("x1").innerHTML = x[0];
document.getElementById("x2").innerHTML = x[1];
document.getElementById("x3").innerHTML = x[2];

x.push(4);
document.getElementById("x4").innerHTML = x[3];

</script>
</body>
</html>
```

With this program, the output is as follows:

JavaScript Program

1

2

3

4

Another way to add elements is through the index number of the array. Let's look at an example of this.

Example 38: The following program shows how to add elements to the array via the index number.

```
<!DOCTYPE html>
<html>
<body>
  <h2>JavaScript Program</h2>

    <p id="x1"></p>
    <p id="x2"></p>
    <p id="x3"></p>
    <p id="x4"></p>

<script>
var x=[1,2,3];

document.getElementById("x1").innerHTML = x[0];
document.getElementById("x2").innerHTML = x[1];
document.getElementById("x3").innerHTML = x[2];

x[3]=4;
document.getElementById("x4").innerHTML = x[3];

</script>
</body>
</html>
```

With this program, the output is as follows:

JavaScript Program

1

2

3

4

You can also add elements to an array if the values are of the 'string' type. Let's look at an example of this.

Example 39: The following program shows how to add elements to the array via the index number when the values are strings.

```
<!DOCTYPE html>
<html>
<body>
 <h2>JavaScript Program</h2>

  <p id="x1"></p>
  <p id="x2"></p>
  <p id="x3"></p>
  <p id="x4"></p>

<script>
var x=["demo1","demo2","demo3"];

document.getElementById("x1").innerHTML = x[0];
document.getElementById("x2").innerHTML = x[1];
document.getElementById("x3").innerHTML = x[2];

x[3]="demo4";
document.getElementById("x4").innerHTML = x[3];

</script>
</body>
</html>
```

62

With this program, the output is as follows:

JavaScript Program

demo1
demo2
demo3
demo4

6.4 Array Methods

Let's look at the various methods available for arrays in more detail. The table below showcases the different methods available for arrays.

Table 1: Arrays Methods

Method	Description
toString()	This method is used to convert an array to a string
join()	This joins all array elements into a string
pop()	This method is used to remove elements from an array
shift()	This removes the first array element and "shifts" all other elements to a lower index
unshift()	This adds a new element to an array and "unshifts" older elements
splice()	This can be used to add new items to an array

Method	Description
concat()	This method can be used to merge arrays
slice()	This "slices" out a piece of an array into a new array
fill()	This is used to fill an array with a static value
forEach()	This calls a provided function once for each element in an array, in order.
copyWithin()	This copies array elements within the array, to and from specified positions
every()	This checks if all elements in an array passes a test
indexOf()	This searches the array for an element, starting at the end, and returns its position
reverse()	This reverses the order of the elements of an array

6.4.1 toString() Method

This method is used to convert an array to a string. Let's look at an example of this function.

Example 40: The following program is used to showcase how to use the toString() method.

```
<!DOCTYPE html>
<html>
<body>
  <h2>JavaScript Program</h2>

    <p id="demo"></p>

<script>
var x=["demo1","demo2","demo3"];

document.getElementById("demo").innerHTML = x.toString();

</script>
</body>
</html>
```

With this program, the output is as follows:

JavaScript Program

demo1,demo2,demo3

6.4.2 join() Method

The join() method joins all array elements into a single string. It behaves similar to the function 'toString()', but in addition you can specify the separator. Let's now look at an example of this function.

Example 41: The following program is used to showcase how to use the join() method

```
<!DOCTYPE html>
<html>
<body>
  <h2>JavaScript Program</h2>

    <p id="demo"></p>

<script>
var x=["demo1","demo2","demo3"];

document.getElementById("demo").innerHTML = x.join("*");

</script>
</body>
</html>
```

With this program, the output is as follows:

JavaScript Program

demo1*demo2*demo3

6.4.3 pop() Method

The pop() method is used to remove elements from an array. Let's now look at an example of this function.

Example 42: The following program is used to showcase how to use the pop() method

```
<!DOCTYPE html>
<html>
<body>
```

```
  <h2>JavaScript Program</h2>

   <p id="demo"></p>
   <p id="demonew"></p>
<script>
var x=["demo1","demo2","demo3"];

document.getElementById("demo").innerHTML = x.toString()
x.pop();
document.getElementById("demonew").innerHTML = x.toString()
</script>
</body>
</html>
```

With this program, the output is as follows:

JavaScript Program

demo1,demo2,demo3

demo1,demo2

6.4.4 shift() Method

The shift() method removes the first array element and "shifts" all other elements to a lower index. Let's now look at an example of this function.

Example 43: The following program is used to showcase how to use the shift() method.

```
<!DOCTYPE html>
<html>
<body>
  <h2>JavaScript Program</h2>
```

```
  <p id="demo"></p>
  <p id="demonew"></p>
<script>
var x=["demo1","demo2","demo3"];

document.getElementById("demo").innerHTML = x.toString()
x.shift();
document.getElementById("demonew").innerHTML = x.toString()
</script>
</body>
</html>
```

With this program, the output is as follows:

JavaScript Program

demo1,demo2,demo3

demo1,demo2

6.4.5 unshift() Method

The unshift() method adds a new element to an array, and "unshifts" older elements. Let's now look at an example of this function.

Example 44: The following program is used to showcase how to use the unshift() method.

```
<!DOCTYPE html>
<html>
<body>
  <h2>JavaScript Program</h2>

  <p id="demo"></p>
  <p id="demonew"></p>
```

```
<script>
var x=["demo1","demo2","demo3"];

document.getElementById("demo").innerHTML = x.toString()
x.unshift("demo4");
document.getElementById("demonew").innerHTML = x.toString()
</script>
</body>
</html>
```

With this program, the output is as follows:

JavaScript Program

demo1,demo2,demo3

demo1,demo2,demo3,demo4

6.4.6 splice() Method

The splice() method can be used to add new items to an array. Let's now look at an example of this function.

Example 45: The following program is used to showcase how to use the splice() method.

```
<!DOCTYPE html>
<html>
<body>
  <h2>JavaScript Program</h2>

    <p id="demo"></p>
    <p id="demonew"></p>
<script>
var x=["demo1","demo2","demo3"];
```

```
document.getElementById("demo").innerHTML = x.toString()
x.splice(2,0,"demo4","demo5");

document.getElementById("demonew").innerHTML = x.toString()
</script>
</body>
</html>
```

The following things need to be noted about the above program:

- The first parameter (2) defines the position where new elements should be added.

- The second parameter (0) defines how many elements should be removed.

With this program, the output is as follows:

JavaScript Program

demo1,demo2,demo3

demo1,demo2,demo4,demo5,demo3

The splice method can also be used to remove elements from the array. Let's look at an example of this.

Example 46: The following program is used to showcase how to use the splice() method to remove elements.

```
<!DOCTYPE html>
<html>
<body>
 <h2>JavaScript Program</h2>
```

```
  <p id="demo"></p>
  <p id="demonew"></p>
<script>
var x=["demo1","demo2","demo3"];

document.getElementById("demo").innerHTML = x.toString()
x.splice(0,1);

document.getElementById("demonew").innerHTML = x.toString()
</script>
</body>
</html>
```

With this program, the output is as follows:

JavaScript Program

demo1,demo2,demo3

demo2,demo3

6.4.7 concat() Method

The concat() method can be used to merge arrays. Let's look at an example of this function.

Example 47: The following program is used to showcase how to use the concat() method.

```
<!DOCTYPE html>
<html>
<body>
 <h2>JavaScript Program</h2>

  <p id="FirstArray"></p>
  <p id="SecondArray"></p>
```

```
    <p id="Combined"></p>

<script>
var x=["demo1","demo2","demo3"];
var y=["demo4","demo5","demo6"];

document.getElementById("FirstArray").innerHTML = x.toString()
document.getElementById("SecondArray").innerHTML =
y.toString()

document.getElementById("Combined").innerHTML = x.concat(y);
</script>
</body>
</html>
```

With this program, the output is as follows:

JavaScript Program

demo1,demo2,demo3

demo4,demo5,demo6

demo1,demo2,demo3, demo4,demo5,demo6

You can also merge multiple arrays using the concat() method. Let's look at an example.

Example 48: The following program shows how to use the concat() method to merge multiple arrays.

```
<!DOCTYPE html>
<html>
<body>
  <h2>JavaScript Program</h2>

    <p id="FirstArray"></p>
```

```
    <p id="SecondArray"></p>
    <p id="ThirdArray"></p>

    <p id="Combined"></p>

<script>
var x=["demo1","demo2","demo3"];
var y=["demo4","demo5","demo6"];
var z=["demo7","demo8","demo9"];

document.getElementById("FirstArray").innerHTML = x.toString()
document.getElementById("SecondArray").innerHTML =
y.toString()
document.getElementById("ThirdArray").innerHTML =
y.toString()

document.getElementById("Combined").innerHTML =
x.concat(y,z);
</script>
</body>
</html>
```

With this program, the output is as follows:

JavaScript Program

demo1,demo2,demo3

demo4,demo5,demo6

demo7,demo8,demo9

demo1,demo2,demo3,demo4,demo5,demo6,demo7,demo8,

demo9

You can also use the concat() function to merge new values to an array. Let's look at an example of this.

Example 49: The following program shows how to use the concat() method to concat values to an array.

```
<!DOCTYPE html>
<html>
<body>
 <h2>JavaScript Program</h2>

  <p id="FirstArray"></p>
  <p id="Combined"></p>

<script>
var x=["demo1","demo2","demo3"];

document.getElementById("FirstArray").innerHTML = x.toString()
document.getElementById("Combined").innerHTML =
x.concat("demo4","demo5");
</script>
</body>
</html>
```

With this program, the output is as follows:

JavaScript Program

demo1,demo2,demo3

demo1,demo2,demo3,demo4,demo5

6.4.8 slice() Method

The slice() method slices out a piece of an array into a new array. Let's now look at an example of this function.

Example 50: The following program is used to showcase how to use the slice() method.

```
<!DOCTYPE html>
<html>
<body>
 <h2>JavaScript Program</h2>

  <p id="FirstArray"></p>
  <p id="Slice"></p>

<script>
var x=["demo1","demo2","demo3","demo4","demo5"];
var y=x.slice(2);
document.getElementById("FirstArray").innerHTML = x.toString()
document.getElementById("Slice").innerHTML = y.toString();
</script>
</body>
</html>
```

With this program, the output is as follows:

JavaScript Program

demo1,demo2,demo3,demo4,demo5

demo3,demo4,demo5

Another variation of the slice() method is where the first parameter can be used to identify the position from where to slice the array from.

Example 51: The following program shows how to use another variation of the slice() method.

```
<!DOCTYPE html>
<html>
<body>
 <h2>JavaScript Program</h2>

  <p id="FirstArray"></p>
  <p id="Slice"></p>

<script>
var x=["demo1","demo2","demo3","demo4","demo5"];
var y=x.slice(2,5);
document.getElementById("FirstArray").innerHTML = x.toString()
document.getElementById("Slice").innerHTML = y.toString();
</script>
</body>
</html>
```

With this program, the output is as follows:

JavaScript Program

demo1,demo2,demo3,demo4,demo5

demo3,demo4,demo5

6.4.9 fill() Method

The fill() method is used to fill an array with a static value. Let's now look at an example of this function.

Example 52: The following program is used to showcase how to use the fill() method.

```
<!DOCTYPE html>
<html>
<body>
 <h2>JavaScript Program</h2>

  <p id="FirstArray"></p>
  <p id="new"></p>

<script>
var x=["demo1","demo2","demo3"];
document.getElementById("FirstArray").innerHTML = x.toString()
x.fill("default");
document.getElementById("new").innerHTML = x.toString();
</script>
</body>
</html>
```

With this program, the output is as follows:

JavaScript Program

demo1,demo2,demo3

default, default, default

6.4.10 forEach() Method

The forEach() method calls a provided function once for each element in an array, in order. Let's now look at an example of this function.

77

Example 53: The following program is used to showcase how to use the forEach() method.

```
<!DOCTYPE html>
<html>
<body>
 <h2>JavaScript Program</h2>

  <p id="FirstArray"></p>
  <p id="new"></p>

<script>
var x=[1,2,3];
var text="";
function myFunction(value)
{
  text+=value;
}
x.forEach(myFunction);
document.getElementById("new").innerHTML = text;
</script>
</body>
</html>
```

In the above program, the following things need to be noted:

- First we define a function called myFunction which appends each value of the array to the text value.

- We then use the forEach method and specify the function to be called.

- The fucntion has the facility to take in each value of the array as a parameter.

78

With this program, the output is as follows:

JavaScript Program

123

6.4.11 copyWithin() Method

The copyWithin() method copies array elements within the array, to and from specified positions. Let's now look at an example of this function.

Example 54: The following program is used to showcase how to use the copyWithin() method.

```
<!DOCTYPE html>
<html>
<body>
  <h2>JavaScript Program</h2>

    <p id="new"></p>

<script>
var x=["demo1","demo2","demo3","demo4"];

x.copyWithin(1,3);
document.getElementById("new").innerHTML = x.toString();
</script>
</body>
</html>
```

With this program, the output is as follows:

JavaScript Program
demo1,demo4,demo3,demo4

6.4.12 every() Method

The every() method checks if all elements in an array passes a specified test. Let's now look at an example of this function.

Example 55: The following program is used to showcase how to use the every() method.

```
<!DOCTYPE html>
<html>
<body>
 <h2>JavaScript Program</h2>

  <p id="new"></p>

<script>

var x=[1,2,3,4];
function Check(value)
{
 return (value>2);
}

document.getElementById("new").innerHTML = x.every(Check);
</script>
</body>
</html>
```

The following things need to be noted about the above program:

- The purpose of this program is to check whether all the elements in the array have a value greater than 2.

- The condition to check if every value is greater than 2 is provided in the function called 'Check'.

80

- The function is then passed to the every() method of the array.

With this program, the output is as follows:

JavaScript Program

false

6.4.13 indexOf() Method

The indexOf() method searches the array for an element, starting at the end, and returns its position. Let's now look at an example of this function.

Example 56: The following program is used to showcase how to use the indexOf() method.

```
<!DOCTYPE html>
<html>
<body>
 <h2>JavaScript Program</h2>

  <p id="new"></p>

<script>

var x=[1,2,3,4];

document.getElementById("new").innerHTML = x.indexOf(2);
</script>
</body>
</html>
```

With this program, the output is as follows:

JavaScript Program

1

6.4.14 reverse() Method

The reverse() method reverses the order of the elements of an array. Let's now look at an example of this function.

Example 57: The following program is used to showcase how to use the reverse() method.

```
<!DOCTYPE html>
<html>
<body>
  <h2>JavaScript Program</h2>

   <p id="new"></p>

<script>

var x=[1,2,3,4];

document.getElementById("new").innerHTML =
x.reverse().toString();
</script>
</body>
</html>
```

With this program, the output is as follows:

JavaScript Program

4,3,2,1

7. Comparisons

Comparisons are used to compare values of data types, which is especially useful in conditions and loops in JavaScript. Let's look in detail at the various comparison operators available. The table below showcases the different comparisons available.

Table 2: Comparison Operators

Operator	Description
==	This is the equal to operator
===	This is the equal value and equal type
!=	This is the not equal to operator
!==	This is the not equal value or not equal type
>	This is the greater than operator
>=	This is the greater and equal to than operator
<	This is the less than operator
<=	This is the less and equal to than operator

Now let's look at an example of these operators

Example 58: The following program is used to showcase how to use the comparison operators.

```
<!DOCTYPE html>
<html>
<body>
 <h2>JavaScript Program</h2>

  <p id="demo1"></p>
  <p id="demo2"></p>
  <p id="demo3"></p>
  <p id="demo4"></p>
  <p id="demo5"></p>
  <p id="demo6"></p>
  <p id="demo7"></p>
  <p id="demo8"></p>
<script>

var x=2;
var y=5;

document.getElementById("demo1").innerHTML = x==y;
document.getElementById("demo2").innerHTML = x!=y;
document.getElementById("demo3").innerHTML = x===y;
document.getElementById("demo4").innerHTML = x!==y;
document.getElementById("demo5").innerHTML = x>y;
document.getElementById("demo6").innerHTML = x>=y;
document.getElementById("demo7").innerHTML = x<y;
document.getElementById("demo8").innerHTML = x<=y;

</script>
</body>
</html>
```

With this program, the output is as follows:

JavaScript Program

false
true
false
true
false
false
true
true

7.1 Conditional (Ternary) Operator

JavaScript also contains a conditional operator that assigns a value to a variable based on a specified condition.

The syntax of the ternary operator is shown below.

```
variablename = (condition) ? value1:value2
```

If the condition is evaluated to true, the variable will be assigned the value1, else it will be assigned value2. Let's look at an example of this.

Example 59: The following program is used to showcase how to use the ternary operator.

```
<!DOCTYPE html>
<html>
<body>
  <h2>JavaScript Program</h2>

  <p id="demo"></p>
```

```
<script>
var x=2;

var status = (x < 5) ? "Value is less than 5":"Value is more than 5";
document.getElementById("demo").innerHTML = status;

</script>
</body>
</html>
```

With this program, the output is as follows:

JavaScript Program

Value is less than 5

The comparison operator can also be used for different data types, meaning the data types on the left and right hand side of the operation can be different. The results can, however, vary and caution should be taken when performing such comparisons.

Example 60: The following program shows how to use comparison operators for different data types.

```
<!DOCTYPE html>
<html>
<body>
 <h2>JavaScript Program</h2>
   <p id="demo"></p>
   <p id="demo1"></p>

<script>
document.getElementById("demo").innerHTML = (5<"10");
document.getElementById("demo1").innerHTML = ("5">"10");
```

```
</script>
</body>
</html>
```

With this program, the output is as follows:

JavaScript Program

true

true

8. Iterators

Iterators are normally used to iterate through the values of a collection, which makes it easier to access the values of the collection. The iterator can be used in the 'for.of' loop statement. The syntax of this is shown below.

```
for (let value of myIterable) {
{
// Execute Code
}
```

Where 'myIterable' is the collection through which the values need to be iterated and 'value' is each value in the collection.

Let's look at an example so that we can see this in further detail.

Example 61: The following program is used to showcase how to use the iterators in JavaScript.

```
<!DOCTYPE html>
<html>
<body>
 <h2>JavaScript Program</h2>

  <p id="demo"></p>
```

```
<script>
var x=[1,2,3,4];
var text="";
for (let value of x) {
  text+=value;
}

document.getElementById("demo").innerHTML = text;

</script>
</body>
</html>
```

With this program, the output is as follows:

JavaScript Program

1234

Another example of using iterators is shown below.

Example 62: The following program shows another example of how to use the iterators in JavaScript.

```
<!DOCTYPE html>
<html>
<body>
  <h2>JavaScript Program</h2>

    <p id="demo"></p>


  <script>

  var text="";
  for (let value of [1,2,3,4]) {
```

```
    text+=value;
}

document.getElementById("demo").innerHTML = text;

</script>
</body>
</html>
```

With this program, the output is as follows::

JavaScript Program

1234

The iterators can also be used for the 'string' data type. Let's look at an example of this.

Example 63: The following program shows another example of how to use the iterators in JavaScript with the string data types.

```
<!DOCTYPE html>
<html>
<body>
  <h2>JavaScript Program</h2>

  <p id="demo"></p>


<script>

var text="";
for (let value of "hello") {
  text+=value;
}
```

```
document.getElementById("demo").innerHTML = text;

</script>
</body>
</html>
```

With this program, the output is as follows:

JavaScript Program

Hello

9. Maps and Sets

The map class is used to hold a set of key value pairs. The values can be primitive types (like numbers or strings) or object types. The syntax for declaring the map object is shown below.

```
var mapname=new Map();
```

Where 'mapname' is the name of the new map object. To add a key value pair to the Map, you can use the 'set' method as shown below.

```
mapname.set(key,value)
```

Where 'key' is the key for the key value pair and 'value' is the subsequent value for the key. To get a value from the map, we can use the 'get' method to get the value for the subsequent key.

Let's look at a way maps can be used through an example.

Example 64: The following program is used to showcase how to use a map class in JavaScript.

```
<!DOCTYPE html>
<html>
<body>
 <h2>JavaScript Program</h2>

  <p id="demo"></p>


<script>

var map=new Map();
map.set("key1","value1");

document.getElementById("demo").innerHTML = "The value for
key1 is "+map.get("key1");

</script>
</body>
</html>
```

The following things need to be noted about the above program:

- We first declare a map object by using the 'new' clause and using the 'map' class.

- Next we set a key/value pair by using the 'set' method.

- Finally we display the value for the key by using the 'get' method.

With this program, the output is as follows:

JavaScript Program
The value for key1 is value1

Let's look at another example of using maps, this time using multiple keys and values.

Example 65: This program shows how to use a map class with multiple key value pairs.

```
<!DOCTYPE html>
<html>
<body>
  <h2>JavaScript Program</h2>

    <p id="demo1"></p>
    <p id="demo2"></p>
    <p id="demo3"></p>


<script>

var map=new Map();
map.set("key1","value1");
map.set("key2","value2");
map.set("key3","value3");

document.getElementById("demo1").innerHTML = "The value for
key1 is "+map.get("key1");
document.getElementById("demo2").innerHTML = "The value for
key2 is "+map.get("key2");
document.getElementById("demo3").innerHTML = "The value for
key3 is "+map.get("key3");
</script>
</body>
</html>
```

With this program, the output is as follows:

JavaScript Program

The value for key1 is value1

The value for key2 is value2

The value for key3 is value3

There are multiple methods available for the map class. Let's look at them in more detail.

Table 3: Map Properties and Methods

Property	Description
size	This is used to display the number of elements in the map
clear	This is used to clear all the elements in the map
delete	This is used to delete an element in the map
has	This is used to check if a map has a particular element or not
keys	This is used to get the keys of the map collection
values	This is used to get the values of the map collection

9.1 size Property

The 'size' property is used to display the number of elements in the map. Let's now look at an example of this property.

Example 66: The following program is used to showcase how to use the size property.

```
<!DOCTYPE html>
<html>
<body>
  <h2>JavaScript Program</h2>

    <p id="demo1"></p>


<script>

var map=new Map();
map.set("key1","value1");
map.set("key2","value2");
map.set("key3","value3");

document.getElementById("demo1").innerHTML = "The number of
elements in the map "+map.size;
</script>
</body>
</html>
```

With this program, the output is as follows:

JavaScript Program

The number of elements in the map 3

9.2 clear Method

The 'clear' method is used to clear all the elements in the map. Let's now look at an example of this method.

Example 67: The following program is used to showcase how to use the clear method.

```
<!DOCTYPE html>
<html>
<body>
 <h2>JavaScript Program</h2>

  <p id="demo1"></p>
  <p id="demo2"></p>

<script>

var map=new Map();
map.set("key1","value1");
map.set("key2","value2");
map.set("key3","value3");

document.getElementById("demo1").innerHTML = "The number of
elements in the map "+map.size;
map.clear();
document.getElementById("demo2").innerHTML = "The number
of elements in the map "+map.size;

</script>
</body>
</html>
```

With this program, the output is as follows:

JavaScript Program

The number of elements in the map 3

The number of elements in the map 0

9.3 delete Method

The 'delete' method is used to delete an element in the map. Let's now look at an example of this method.

Example 68: The following program is used to showcase how to use the delete method.

```
<!DOCTYPE html>
<html>
<body>
  <h2>JavaScript Program</h2>

  <p id="demo1"></p>
  <p id="demo2"></p>

<script>

var map=new Map();
map.set("key1","value1");
map.set("key2","value2");
map.set("key3","value3");

document.getElementById("demo1").innerHTML = "The number of
elements in the map "+map.size;
map.delete("key2");
document.getElementById("demo2").innerHTML = "The number
of elements in the map "+map.size;
```

```
</script>
</body>
</html>
```

With this program, the output is as follows:

JavaScript Program

The number of elements in the map 3

The number of elements in the map 2

9.4 has Method

The 'has' method is used to check if a map has a particular element or not. Let's now look at an example of this method.

Example 69: The following program is used to showcase how to use the has method.

```
<!DOCTYPE html>
<html>
<body>
 <h2>JavaScript Program</h2>

  <p id="demo1"></p>
  <p id="demo2"></p>

<script>

var map=new Map();
map.set("key1","value1");
map.set("key2","value2");
map.set("key3","value3");

document.getElementById("demo1").innerHTML = "The number of
```

```
elements in the map "+map.size;

document.getElementById("demo2").innerHTML = "Does the map
have the element key2 " +map.has("key2");

</script>
</body>
</html>
```

With this program, the output is as follows:

JavaScript Program

The number of elements in the map 3

Does the map have the element key2 true

9.5 keys Method

The 'keys' method is used to acquire the keys of the map
collection. Let's now look at an example of this method.

Example 70: The following program is used to showcase how to use the keys method.

```
<!DOCTYPE html>
<html>
<body>
 <h2>JavaScript Program</h2>

   <p id="demo1"></p>

<script>

var map=new Map();
map.set("key1","value1");
```

```
map.set("key2","value2");
map.set("key3","value3");

var text="";
for (var key of map.keys())
 {
   text+=key;
   text+="</br>";
 }
document.getElementById("demo1").innerHTML = text;

</script>
</body>
</html>
```

With this program, the output is as follows:

JavaScript Program

key1
key2
key3

9.6 values Method

The 'values' method is used to get the values of the map collection. Let's now look at an example of this method.

Example 71: The following program is used to showcase how to use the values method.

```
<!DOCTYPE html>
<html>
<body>
  <h2>JavaScript Program</h2>
```

```
    <p id="demo1"></p>

<script>

var map=new Map();
map.set("key1","value1");
map.set("key2","value2");
map.set("key3","value3");

var text="";
for (var value of map.values())
 {
  text+= value;
  text+="</br>";
 }
document.getElementById("demo1").innerHTML = text;

</script>
</body>
</html>
```

With this program, the output is as follows:

JavaScript Program

value1
value2
value3

9.7 set Class

The 'set' class lets you store unique values of any type. The values can be primitive types, such as numbers and strings, or object types. The syntax for declaring the 'set' object is shown below.

```
var setname=new Set();
```

Where 'setname' is the name of the new set object. To add a value to the set, you can use the 'add' method as shown below.

```
setname.add(value)
```

To check whether the set has a value we can use the 'has' method. Let's look at a way sets can be used through an example.

Example 72: This program is used to show how to use a set class in JavaScript.

```
<!DOCTYPE html>
<html>
<body>
 <h2>JavaScript Program</h2>

  <p id="demo1"></p>

<script>

var set=new Set();
set.add("value1");
set.add("value2");
set.add("value3");

var text="";
document.getElementById("demo1").innerHTML = "Does the set
contain value2 "+set.has("value2");

</script>
</body>
</html>
```

With this program, the output is as follows:

JavaScript Program

Does the set contain value2 true

Table 4: Set Properties and Methods

Property	Description
size	This is used to display the number of elements in the set
clear	This is used to clear all the elements in the map
delete	This is used to delete an element in the map
values	This is used to get the values of the map collection

9.8 size Property

The 'size' property is used to display the number of elements in the set. Let's look at an example of this property.

Example 73: The following program is used to showcase how to use the size property.

```
<!DOCTYPE html>
<html>
<body>
 <h2>JavaScript Program</h2>

  <p id="demo1"></p>
```

```
<script>

var set=new Set();
set.add("value1");
set.add("value2");
set.add("value3");

var text="";
document.getElementById("demo1").innerHTML = "The number of
elements is "+ set.size;

</script>
</body>
</html>
```

With this program, the output is as follows:

JavaScript Program

The number of elements is 3

9.9 clear Method

The 'clear' method is used to clear all the elements in the set.
Let's now look at an example of this method.

Example 74: The following program is used to showcase how to use the clear method.

```
<!DOCTYPE html>
<html>
<body>
  <h2>JavaScript Program</h2>

    <p id="demo1"></p>
```

```
    <p id="demo2"></p>
<script>

var set=new Set();
set.add("value1");
set.add("value2");
set.add("value3");

document.getElementById("demo1").innerHTML = "The number of
elements is "+ set.size;
set.clear();
document.getElementById("demo2").innerHTML = "The number
of elements is "+ set.size;
</script>
</body>
</html>
```

With this program, the output is as follows:

JavaScript Program

The number of elements is 3

The number of elements is 0

9.10 delete Method

The 'delete' method is used to delete an element in the set. Let's now look at an example of this method.

Example 75: The following program is used to showcase how to use the delete method.

```
<!DOCTYPE html>
<html>
<body>
```

```
  <h2>JavaScript Program</h2>

  <p id="demo1"></p>
  <p id="demo2"></p>
<script>

var set=new Set();
set.add("value1");
set.add("value2");
set.add("value3");

document.getElementById("demo1").innerHTML = "The number of
elements is "+ set.size;
set.delete("value2");
document.getElementById("demo2").innerHTML = "The number
of elements is "+ set.size;
</script>
</body>
</html>
```

With this program, the output is as follows:

JavaScript Program

The number of elements is 3

The number of elements is 2

9.11 values Method

The 'values' method is used to get the values of the set collection. Let's quickly look at an example of this method.

Example 76: The following program is used to showcase how to use the values method.

```
<!DOCTYPE html>
<html>
<body>
  <h2>JavaScript Program</h2>

    <p id="demo1"></p>

<script>

var set=new Set();
set.add("value1");
set.add("value2");
set.add("value3");

var text="";
for (var value of set.values())
  {
   text+=value;
   text+="</br>";
  }

document.getElementById("demo1").innerHTML = text;
</script>
</body>
</html>
```

With this program, the output is as follows:

JavaScript Program

value1

value2

value3

10. Objects and Properties

Objects can be used in JavaScript to hold properties, and values for those properties. For example, if we wanted to store information about students in our program, we can do so with the help of objects and properties.

An object can be defined directly in JavaScript by means of curly braces and using the object property and value defined for the object. The syntax is shown below.

```
var objectname={propertyname1:propertyvalue1...}
```

Where 'objectname' is the name of the object and 'propertyname1' and 'propertyvalue1' is for defining the property and value of the property. Let's now look at an example of how this works.

Example 77: The following program is used to showcase how to use objects.

```
<!DOCTYPE html>
<html>
<body>
  <h2>JavaScript Program</h2>

  <p id="ID"></p>
  <p id="name"></p>
```

```
<script>

var student={id:1,name:"Joe"}

document.getElementById("ID").innerHTML = student.id;
document.getElementById("name").innerHTML = student.name;
</script>
</body>
</html>
```

Things to note about the above program:

- We define an object called 'student' with 2 key values. The first key value is id:1 and the other is name:"Joe".

- We can then access the key via the dot operator on the object.

With this program, the output is as follows:

JavaScript Program

1

Joe

We are also able to define multiple objects. Let's look an example of this.

Example 78: The following program is used to showcase how to use multiple objects.

```
<!DOCTYPE html>
<html>
<body>
  <h2>JavaScript Program</h2>

    <p id="ID1"></p>
```

```
    <p id="name1"></p>

    <p id="ID2"></p>
    <p id="name2"></p>

<script>

var student1={id:1,name:"Joe"}
var student2={id:2,name:"Mark"}

document.getElementById("ID1").innerHTML = student1.id;
document.getElementById("name1").innerHTML = student1.name;

document.getElementById("ID2").innerHTML = student2.id;
document.getElementById("name2").innerHTML =
student2.name;

</script>
</body>
</html>
```

With this program, the output is as follows:

JavaScript Program

1

Joe

2

Mark

We are able to change the values of the properties during the course of the program as well. Let's look at an example on this.

Example 79: The following program is used to showcase how to change the properties of an object.

```
<!DOCTYPE html>
<html>
<body>
 <h2>JavaScript Program</h2>

  <p id="ID1"></p>
  <p id="name1"></p>

  <p id="ID2"></p>
  <p id="name2"></p>

  <p id="ID3"></p>
  <p id="name3"></p>

<script>

var student1={id:1,name:"Joe"}
var student2={id:2,name:"Mark"}

document.getElementById("ID1").innerHTML = student1.id;
document.getElementById("name1").innerHTML = student1.name;

document.getElementById("ID2").innerHTML = student2.id;
document.getElementById("name2").innerHTML =
student2.name;

student2.id=3;
student2.name="John";

document.getElementById("ID3").innerHTML = student2.id;
document.getElementById("name3").innerHTML =
student2.name;
```

```
</script>
</body>
</html>
```

With this program, the output is as follows:

JavaScript Program

1
Joe
2
Mark
3
John

You can also use the 'new Object' keyword to create a new object. Let's look at an example shown below.

Example 80: The following program is used to showcase how to use the new object keyword.

```
<!DOCTYPE html>
<html>
<body>
  <h2>JavaScript Program</h2>

    <p id="ID1"></p>
    <p id="name1"></p>

    <p id="ID2"></p>
    <p id="name2"></p>

    <p id="ID3"></p>
    <p id="name3"></p>
<script>
```

```
var student1=new Object();
student1.id=1;
student1.name="Joe";

var student2=new Object();
student2.id=2;
student2.name="Mark";

document.getElementById("ID1").innerHTML = student1.id;
document.getElementById("name1").innerHTML = student1.name;

document.getElementById("ID2").innerHTML = student2.id;
document.getElementById("name2").innerHTML =
student2.name;

student2.id=3;
student2.name="John";

document.getElementById("ID3").innerHTML = student2.id;
document.getElementById("name3").innerHTML =
student2.name;

</script>
</body>
</html>
```

With this program, the output is as follows:

JavaScript Program

1
Joe
2
Mark
3
John

10.1 Object Constructor

In JavaScript, a function can be used as a constructor for an object. This helps in creating multiple objects of the same type. The syntax is shown below.

```
function functionname(propertyvalue)
{
this.propertyname= propertyvalue;
}
var newobject = new functionname();
```

Here, the 'functionname' acts as the constructor and the objects are created based on the function.

Next, the function can take in the values which will be assigned to the properties of the object. The values can be assigned to the 'propertyname' with the help of the 'this' operator. The 'this' operator is used to address the current object being accessed by the function.

Let's now look at this through an example.

Example 81: The following program is used to showcase how to use functions to create objects.

```
<!DOCTYPE html>
<html>
<body>
  <h2>JavaScript Program</h2>

  <p id="ID1"></p>
  <p id="name1"></p>

  <p id="ID2"></p>
  <p id="name2"></p>
```

```
<script>
function Student(id,name)
{
  this.id=id;
  this.name=name;
}

var student1=new Student(1,"Joe");
var student2=new Student(2,"Mark");

document.getElementById("ID1").innerHTML = student1.id;
document.getElementById("name1").innerHTML = student1.name;

document.getElementById("ID2").innerHTML = student2.id;
document.getElementById("name2").innerHTML =
student2.name;

</script>
</body>
</html>
```

With this program, the output is as follows:

JavaScript Program

1
Joe
2
Mark

The property values can also be changed during the course of the program, just like normal objects. Let's look at an example of this.

Example 82: The following program shows how to use functions to create objects and change the values accordingly.

```
<!DOCTYPE html>
<html>
<body>
  <h2>JavaScript Program</h2>

  <p id="ID1"></p>
  <p id="name1"></p>

  <p id="ID2"></p>
  <p id="name2"></p>

  <p id="ID3"></p>
  <p id="name3"></p>

<script>
function Student(id,name)
{
  this.id=id;
  this.name=name;
}

var student1=new Student(1,"Joe");
var student2=new Student(2,"Mark");

document.getElementById("ID1").innerHTML = student1.id;
document.getElementById("name1").innerHTML = student1.name;

document.getElementById("ID2").innerHTML = student2.id;
document.getElementById("name2").innerHTML =
student2.name;

student2.id=3;
student2.name="John";
```

```
document.getElementById("ID3").innerHTML = student2.id;
document.getElementById("name3").innerHTML =
student2.name;

</script>
</body>
</html>
```

With this program, the output is as follows:

JavaScript Program

1
Joe
2
Mark
3
John

10.2 Looping Through Properties in an Object

The 'for' loop in JaavScript can be used to iterate through the properties of an object. The syntax for this is shown below.

```
for (variable in object) {
//    code to be executed
}
```

Let's now look at an example of this.

Example 83: The following program is used to showcase how to iterate through the properties of an object.

```
<!DOCTYPE html>
<html>
<body>
  <h2>JavaScript Program</h2>

   <p id="demo"></p>

   <script>
   var text="";
function Student(id,name)
{
 this.id=id;
 this.name=name;
}

var student1=new Student(1,"Joe");

for(i in student1)
{
 text+=student1[i];
 text+="</br>";
}
document.getElementById("demo").innerHTML = text;

</script>
</body>
</html>
```

With this program, the output is as follows:

JavaScript Program

1

Joe

10.3 Adding Properties to an Object

Adding properties to an object is really easy and can be done by simply adding a value to the property of the object.

Let's look at an example of this.

Example 84: The following program is used to showcase how to add properties to an object.

```
<!DOCTYPE html>
<html>
<body>
  <h2>JavaScript Program</h2>

    <p id="demo"></p>

    <script>
    var text="";
function Student(id,name)
{
 this.id=id;
 this.name=name;
}

var student1=new Student(1,"Joe");
student1.subject="Math";
for(i in student1)
{
 text+=student1[i];
 text+="</br>";
}
document.getElementById("demo").innerHTML = text;

</script>
</body>
</html>
```

With this program, the output is as follows:

JavaScript Program

1
Joe
Math

10.4 Deleting Properties

Deleting properties of an object is really easy as well and can be done by just using the 'delete' method. The syntax is shown below.

```
delete objectname.propertyname
```

Let's now look at an example of this.

Example 85: The following program is used to showcase how to add properties to an object.

```
<!DOCTYPE html>
<html>
<body>
  <h2>JavaScript Program</h2>

  <p id="demo"></p>

  <script>
  var text="";
function Student(id,name)
{
  this.id=id;
  this.name=name;
}
```

```
var student1=new Student(1,"Joe");
student1.subject="Math";
delete student1.name;
for(i in student1)
{
 text+=student1[i];
 text+="</br>";
}
document.getElementById("demo").innerHTML = text;

</script>
</body>
</html>
```

With this program, the output is as follows:

JavaScript Program

1

Math

11. Methods in JavaScript

JavaScript methods are actions that can be performed on objects. Any property that contains a function becomes a JavaScript method. The syntax of a method is given below.

```
methodName : function() { //Code here }
```

You can then access the method via the object name as shown below.

```
objectName.methodName()
```

Let's look at an example of how to implement a method.

Example 86: The following program is used to showcase how to add JavaScript methods.

```
<!DOCTYPE html>
<html>
<body>
  <h2>JavaScript Program</h2>

  <p id="demo"></p>

  <script>
  var text="";
```

```
var student1={id:1,name:"Mark",Display:function() { return
this.name;}};

document.getElementById("demo").innerHTML =
student1.Display();

</script>
</body>
</html>
```

With this program, the output is as follows:

JavaScript Program

Mark

It becomes easier to declare methods that can be used to
display the properties of an object when using getter methods.
Let's look at an example of this.

Example 87: The following program is used to showcase how to work with JavaScript methods.

```
<!DOCTYPE html>
<html>
<body>
 <h2>JavaScript Program</h2>

  <p id="demo"></p>
  <p id="demo1"></p>

  <script>
  var text="";

var student1={id:1,name:"Mark",
Displayid:function() { return this.id;},
```

```
Displayname:function() { return this.name;},
};

document.getElementById("demo").innerHTML =
student1.Displayid();
document.getElementById("demo1").innerHTML =
student1.Displayname();
</script>
</body>
</html>
```

With this program, the output is as follows:

JavaScript Program

1

Mark

You can also add methods that have logic added to them, in order to make more sense to objects. In the next example we can provide the 'total marks', which can be added to the 'student' object. So let's look at this example and how the above can be done.

Example 88: The following program is used to showcase how to add more JavaScript methods.

```
<!DOCTYPE html>
<html>
<body>
 <h2>JavaScript Program</h2>

  <p id="demo"></p>
  <p id="demo1"></p>
  <p id="demo2"></p>
```

```
<script>
var text="";

var student1={id:1,name:"Mark",
Displayid:function() { return this.id;},
Displayname:function() { return this.name;},
Total:function() {return (this.Subject1+this.Subject2)}
};

document.getElementById("demo").innerHTML =
student1.Displayid();
document.getElementById("demo1").innerHTML =
student1.Displayname();

student1.Subject1=20;
student1.Subject2=40;

document.getElementById("demo2").innerHTML =
student1.Total();
</script>
</body>
</html>
```

With this program, the output is as follows:

JavaScript Program

1

Mark

60

12. Form Handling

The heart of JavaScript has always been the ability to handle HTML forms. This adds a lot of power when working with web applications.

Some examples of where you might want to use form handling are:

- Validating details entered on forms – Let's say you want to validate the details entered on a form such as the email ID or user name, then this can be done with JavaScript.

- Adding elements to tables – If you are displaying a table of values on a form, and want to add elements and show those to the user, then this can be done with JavaScript. Once all the values are entered, the server side scripting could be used to save them to persistent storage.

- Disabling controls on the screen – In situations where you want to disable or hide controls on the screen after an event occurs, this can also be done with JavaScript.

The handling of events is done through functions and event properties, which are available for HTML controls. Let's now look at various examples of how form validation can be done in JavaScript.

Example 89: The following program is used to showcase how to display text when a button is clicked.

```
<!DOCTYPE html>
<html>
<body>
 <h2>JavaScript Program</h2>
 <form>
 <input type="button" id="btn1" value="Click Me"
onclick="Display()">
 <p id=demo></p>
 </form>

  <script>
  function Display()
{
document.getElementById("demo").innerHTML = "Hello World";
}
</script>
</body>
</html>
```

With this program, the output is as follows:

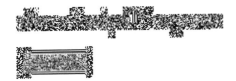

And after the button is clicked, the output is:

130

JavaScript Program

Click Me

Hello World

Now let's look at an example in which we can disable a button upon clicking another button.

Example 90: The following program is used to showcase how to disable a button.

```
<!DOCTYPE html>
<html>
<body>
 <h2>JavaScript Program</h2>
 <form>
 <input type="button" id="btn1" value="Hide Me">
 <input type="button" id="btn2" value="Click Me"
onclick="Display()">

 </form>

  <script>
  function Display()
{
 btn1.disabled=true;
}
</script>
</body>
</html>
```

With this program, the output is as follows:

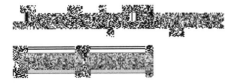

When you click the 'Click Me' button, you will get the below output:

JavaScript Program

Now let's look at an example of displaying all the items present in a combo box that is present in an HTML form.

Example 91: The following program is used to showcase how to display all the values in an option box.

```
<!DOCTYPE html>
<html>
<body>
  <h2>JavaScript Program</h2>
  <form>
   This is the chapters in the tutorial<br>
   <select id="chapters">
   <option>Data Types</option>
   <option>Arrays</option>
   <option>Objects</option>
   <option>Operators</option>
    </select>
```

```
<input type="button" onclick="Display()" value="Display">
<p id="demo"></p>
 </form>

  <script>
  function Display()
{
 var x = document.getElementById("chapters");
   var text = "";
   var i;
   for (i = 0; i < x.length; i++) {
     text = text + " " + x.options[i].text;
     text+="<br>";
   }
   document.getElementById("demo").innerHTML = text;
}
</script>
</body>
</html>
```

With this program, the output is as follows:

JavaScript Program

This is the chapters in the tutorial

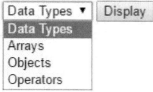

When you click the 'Display' button, the following will be the output:

JavaScript Program

This is the chapters in the tutorial

Data Types ▼ Display

Data Types
Arrays
Objects
Operators

Next we look at an example on how to get the option selected in the options list.

Example 92: The following program is used to showcase how to display the selected value in an option box.

```html
<!DOCTYPE html>
<html>
<body>
 <h2>JavaScript Program</h2>
 <form>
  This is the chapters in the tutorial<br>
  <select id="chapters">
  <option>Data Types</option>
  <option>Arrays</option>
  <option>Objects</option>
  <option>Operators</option>
   </select>
<input type="button" onclick="Display()" value="Display">
<p id="demo"></p>
 </form>

  <script>
  function Display()
{
```

```
  var obj = document.getElementById("chapters");
  document.getElementById("demo").innerHTML =
  obj.options[obj.selectedIndex].text;
}


</script>
</body>
</html>
```

With this program, the output is as follows:

JavaScript Program

This is the chapters in the tutorial

Arrays ▼ | Display

And when you click the 'Display' button, you will get the following:

JavaScript Program

This is the chapters in the tutorial

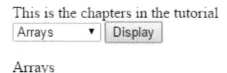

Arrays ▼ | Display

Arrays

We are also able to reset all the controls in a form. Let's look at how that is done through an example.

Example 93: The following program is used to showcase how to reset the controls in a form.

```
<!DOCTYPE html>
<html>
<body>
 <h2>JavaScript Program</h2>
 <form id="frm1">
  Name :         
  <input id="txtName"/><br><br>
  Password :   
  <input id="txtName"/><br>

   </select>
<input type="button" onclick="Reset()" value="Reset">
<p id="demo"></p>
 </form>

  <script>
  function Reset()
{
 document.getElementById("frm1").reset();
}


</script>
</body>
</html>
```

With this program, the output is as follows when you enter a name and password:

JavaScript Program

Name :　　Name

Password :　Password

Reset

And then if you click the 'Reset' button, the output is:

JavaScript Program

Name :

Password :
Reset

Let's look at an example that can be used to submit all the controls in a form.

Example 94: This program is used to show how to submit the controls in a form.

```
<!DOCTYPE html>
<html>
<body>
 <h2>JavaScript Program</h2>
 <form id="frm1">
  Name :         
  <input id="txtName"/><br><br>
  Password :   
  <input id="txtName"/><br>

   </select>
<input type="button" onclick="Submit()" value="Submit">
```

```
<p id="demo"></p>
 </form>

  <script>
  function Submit()
{
 document.getElementById("frm1").submit();
}

</script>
</body>
</html>
```

With this program, the output is as follows if you enter a name and password:

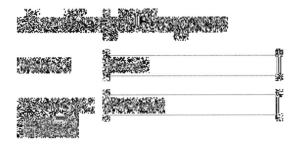

And once you click the 'Submit' button, the output is:

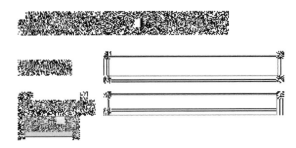

13. Multimedia

JavaScript can be used to work with the multimedia elements in browsers. Let's look at a simple example that can be used to get the names for all the plugins that are loaded in a browser.

Example 95: The following program is used to showcase how to get the plugins in a browser.

```
<!DOCTYPE html>
<html>
<body>
 <h2>JavaScript Program</h2>

<p id="demo"></p>

  <script>
  var text="";
  for (i=0; i<navigator.plugins.length; i++) {

      text+=navigator.plugins[i].name;
      text+="</br>";
    }
document.getElementById("demo").innerHTML=text;
</script>
</body>
</html>
```

With this program, the output is as follows:

JavaScript Program

Widevine Content Decryption Module

Chrome PDF Viewer

Native Client

Chrome PDF Viewer

Next, let's look at an example that can be used to play videos in a browser.

Example 96: The following program is used to showcase how to work with videos in JavaScript.

```
<!DOCTYPE html>
<html>
<body>
 <h2>JavaScript Program</h2>

   <embed id="demo" name="demo"
   src="https://www.youtube.com/embed/Ukg_U3CnJWI"
   width="318" height="300" play="false" loop="false">

   </embed>

   <form name="form" id="form" action="#" method="get">
     <input type="button" value="Start" onclick="play();" />
   </form>
<script>
function play()
     {
       if (!document.demo.IsPlaying()){
         document.demo.Play();
       }
```

```
        }

</script>
  </body>
</html>
```

With this program, the output is as follows:

JavaScript Program

Start

Conclusion

This has brought us to the end of this guide, but it doesn't mean your JavaScript education should end here. If you enjoyed this guide, be sure to continue your journey with the next book in the series, which looks at more advanced topics and techniques while still being beginner friendly.

JAVASCRIPT

Advanced Features and Programming Techniques

a FREE Kindle Version with Paperback

Lastly, this book was written not only to be a teaching guide, but also a reference manual. So remember to always keep it near, as you venture through this wonderful world of programming.

Good luck and happy programming!

About the Author

Nathan Clark is an expert programmer with nearly 20 years of experience in the software industry.

With a master's degree from MIT, he has worked for some of the leading software companies in the United States and built up extensive knowledge of software design and development.

Nathan and his wife, Sarah, started their own development firm in 2009 to be able to take on more challenging and creative projects. Today they assist high-caliber clients from all over the world.

Nathan enjoys sharing his programming knowledge through his book series, developing innovative software solutions for their clients and watching classic sci-fi movies in his free time.

Made in the USA
Middletown, DE
13 January 2019